The Nine Stripes of
Tiger Zeke, Pirate King

Written and illustrated by
Ashley Nebelsieck

Phoenician Foundry, Phoenix Arizona

Phoenician Foundry
Phoenix, Arizona
ISBN 978-1-7349799-5-4
Library of Congress Control Number: 2024906972

For my two little kittens:

Right from the start, I loved your great pirate-king hearts

Table of Contents

Introductions and Origins of the Tail	7
The Tip: Sliding Doors	11
Stripe Eight: The Owl	15
Stripe Seven: Rattlesnakes	19
The Tale of Calico Jack	23
Stripe Six: In-laws and Outlaws	27
Stripes Five and Four: The Banditos	31
Stripe Three: Discrimination	35
Stripe Two: Mutiny!	41
The Final Stripe: The Fall of Fanny	45
Stripe One, Holding: And Pass the Mustard	49
Epilogue: Freedom	53

Introductions and Origins of the Tail

We knew a kitten named Tiger Zeke.
He lived within our walls.
He sat upon our mother's lap
and stalked the baby down our halls.

His coat was tabby ginger
(that's orange, to those less spicy).
He came to us a feral orphan for
Dad thought a Siamese too pricey.

His eyes, they were clear aqua blue,
his whiskers, broad and milky,
but his finest feature of all, by far?
His tail, flaming, long and silky.

He held it high when he walked about.
He twitched it when displeased.
He used it for a pillow when he slept
and a tissue when he sneezed.

It had nine stripes from rump to tip,
nine fluffy golden rings.
If up front, his accents were not-quite-Queens,
arrears, he was fit for kings.

He ate smoked salmon for breakfast,
nipped the baby's bum as he got dressed,
jumped on counters, and darted for doors,
but the one game he liked best

he played each day as we left for school,
when he'd sneak into the nursery
and climb aboard our toy pirate ship
to pretend he was a mercen'ry.

He ate our golden chocolate coins
and stole Teddy's tricot hat,
swung from the curtains whilst squinting an eye—
No pet! He was a pirate cat.

Whatever we thought, he knew in his heart,
he was born running wild and free
under the neon sign of *Autumn Moon*
and a dumpster full of chop-suey.

There he lived with his litter til a terrible rain
swept him clinging to a crate of bok choy,
down the canals and the gutters, straight across town,
thrilled and mewing "Ahoy!"

Oh the sights that he saw! The adventures he had,
three days of braving high seas
munching waterlogged egg rolls and using his tail
to steer his ship and dodge the debris.

He washed upon shore, three feet from our front door,
half-drowned little stripy wanderluster.
We dried him off then cured his cough,
and pronounced him a feline uppercruster.

But nothing we said, no reason could sway him,
not public talk, nor private chat—
that he would be happier safe, indoors.
He was convinced he was a pirate cat!

The Tip: Sliding Doors

We called him Zeke, he called us "matey."
When he purred, it came out like *"arrrr."*
He thieved, he plundered, he plotted escape he
stole the keys to our father's new car.

So I bought him a leash with a little plaid jacket
and took him for a walk outside
to get some sunshine and a bit of fresh air—
A great idea, if not for his pride.

Straight away, he seemed embarrassed
as I dragged him around the yard.
And then to his horror, under the purple sage brush,
he saw a face—rather beautiful—but scarred.

She had tufted ears, and a pink heart-shaped nose,
which she stared down at him like an aristocrat.
She had spots with her stripes, and one yellow eye;
Oh no, she was a real pirate cat!

Zeke about fainted in his smart tartan coat,
disgraced to be seen on a leash.
He went totally limp, so I carried him in
for comfort and a small slice of quiche.

But upon that day and those that soon followed
Tiger Zeke grew calculating and bold.
He bet his tail upon following his heart,
vowing to break out, be released, or paroled.

And then one brisk morning, Zeke made his move
when I went out to pick some Swiss chard.
As I opened the door, he dashed cross the room
to keep him safe, I slammed it—quite hard.

He almost made it out the door,
nearly hit his freedom jackpot.
My eyes, they told me he'd gotten away,
but my ears assured me he did not.

You never heard such a terrible scream,
but he didn't quite give us the slip off.
For though he made it through, body and head,
the door took the tail of his tip off

or the tip of his tail—either way, it was severed,
and how he did holler and cry.
"My tail, my tail, my beautiful tail!"
Beneath the sage, blinked one yellow eye.

To the vet we rushed for a bandage and collar,
for weeks in his cone he did wait.
On the day they unwrapped it,
he counted his stripes,
but there were not nine; there were eight.

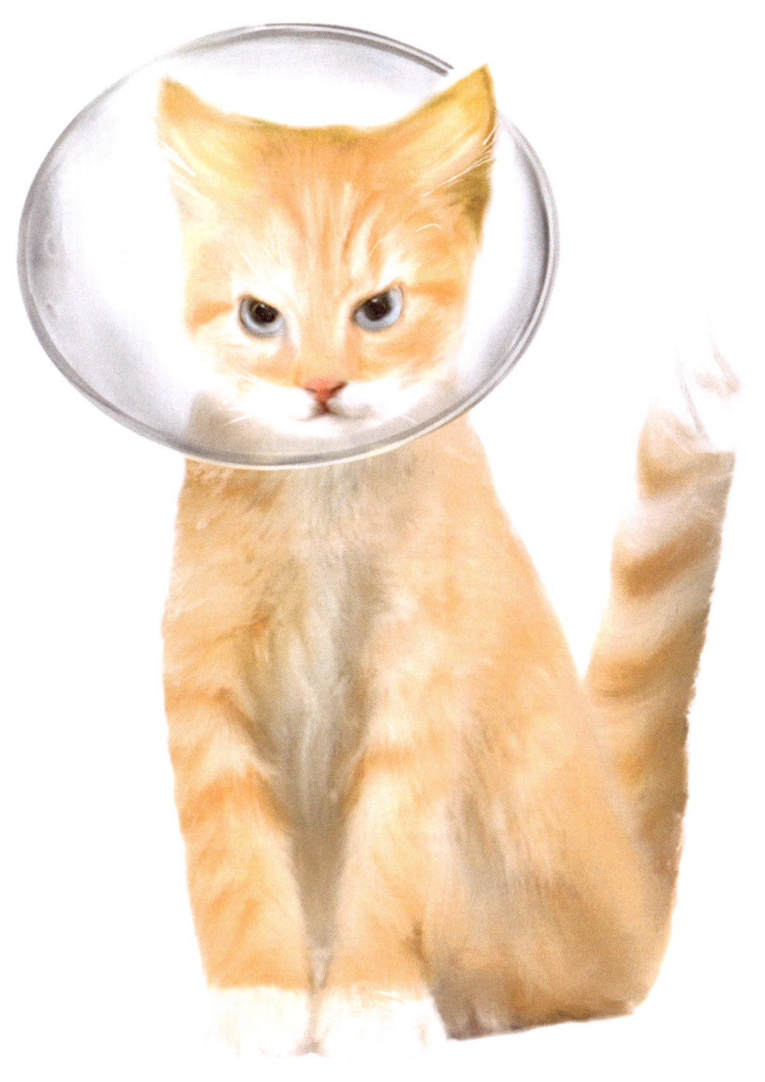

Stripe Eight: The Owl

Any old cat would have given up there
and preserved what was left of his beauty,
but he knew what he was, what he wanted to do,
and doubled his efforts like it was his duty.

The door, 'twas a hazard,
he noted that much was true,
but always the sailor, he just changed his tack
and instead scaled the chimney flue.

Of course, that night we burned no fire:
Zeke wasn't Santa Claus or fireproof.
He just grasped with his claws and held on with his jaws
and climbed all the way up to the roof.

At last he was free! Above him big sky,
stars, moon and the music of the night;
but the dark hid a phantom, as darkness will do,
and elation, it soon turned to fright.

"Look out!" someone squawked, and kitty ducked down
as an owl swooped in, talons and beak.
It aimed for his head, but just knocked off his hat
and instead, hooked the tail of Tiger Zeke.

Now pirates are fighters, and Zeke was also a biter,
and that owl would have loved to let go,
but his talons were stuck in, so he got a quick nip in
Zeke's tail, to release his cargo.

Zeke dropped from the sky and fell through the roof
of the coop of the chicken who saved him.
She bundled him up, and they talked through the night.
"Stay indoors," she tried to persuade him.

She once had three sisters, a beautiful flock,
but the desert was a tough place to forage.
One by one, they went missing at just about dawn,
because coyotes, they do not eat porridge.

So Brownie stayed cooped up, for that was her name,
and "chickens" are not called such for daring;
likewise, the next morning found Zeke under our hen,
in her nest box, both hurt and despairing.

Though Brownie was broody, and Zeke was a cutie,
how he turned up in her clutch, to us, was a mystery.
But when we got him inside and taped up his tail,
we did notice stripe eight now was history.

Stripe Seven: Rattlesnakes

Back at home in his cone, Zeke had a few days ponder
the wise words of our brown Wyandotte.
As he sat on the sill, gazing out at the pool,
he fancied my kayak a slick sailing yacht.

Up the chimney he rose, like the man in red clothes,
as soon as he shook off his collar.
He boarded the boat but before he could push off,
from my bed, I heard a now familiar holler.

Who did Zeke awaken? A sleepy rattlesnake in
his den, who struck with the bite he inflicts.
Too drowsy to contend, the snake started at the wrong end,
and Zeke's seven stripes now were but six.

Before I could save him, a strange cat came to aid him:
the spotty girl from under the brush! Said,
"I'm usually shy but, you make a terrible pirate,"
and she threw the snake off by its head.

A ship may be safe in its harbor,
and a kitten most safe within doors,
but ships, they are built to sail farther,
and Zeke, he was born to explore.

Though his tail grew foreshortened, he thought it important
to make it back out to her that very same night.
He felt he must prove, he had the right pirate moves.
Plus, he believed it was love at third sight.

"Shiver me timbers!"
she said in surprise at Zeke's unexpected reprise,
when he turned up on the roof in his band-aid.
"Yo ho ho," he replied, and caught a gleam in her eye,
"They may take me stripes, but this old salt's not afraid."

In choosing a first mate, for a buccaneer's first date
expect an eyepatch, peg leg, or a hook,
but upon Zeke's pirate honor, the bobtail upon her
was a shock he worked hard to overlook.

The next several nights they spent roaming the ports,
caterwauling and singing sea shanties.
They stole from the rich mice
then stole from the poor mice,
for pirates make poor vigilantes.

They sailed and they plundered,
while Zeke should have slumbered,
but in the back of his mind something stuck in:
Why did he rush back, at dawn's very first crack,
like he would turn into a pumpkin?

Far from a heave-ho,
Zeke's get-up-and-go was a no-show.
Sure, at night, he'd tighten his swashbuckles,
but he spent all his days in a smoked salmon haze.
Honestly, he quite missed the white knuckles.

The Tale of Calico Jack

One night, he wasn't sure that he'd bother at all,
with the chimney cold and dank as Dundee,
but the will deep inside him and scent of chlorine did remind him
that his life, love, and lady was the sea.

But as he followed his nose, a cluck did oppose
his plan to continue his piracy.
"Please," Brownie pleaded, "prudence is needed.
Your *belle* dame is *sans* all *merci*."

Reared 'hind a dumpster, Zeke's French lacked some lustre,
So he failed heed our Hen's poetic warning.
He just strode past her coop and boarded his sloop
to make the most of the pool before morning.

Somewhere in the darkness a coyote yapped
and turned the somber mood quite severe.
The rain started falling, and Fanny began recalling
the most terrible battle of her pirate career:

On a night much like this, with the rain falling down
cornered by a hungry coyote pack,
Fanny fought tooth and nail in the wind and the hail
but alas, was soon to become a midnight snack.

Just then without a sound, Calico Jack came around,
the greatest pirate captain in all desert history!
But to her surprise, he knocked out one of her eyes
when he hit her so hard, she flew into a tree.

Poor Fanny was saved, but now her life must be braved
and viewed through a single amber lens.
The coyotes, they scattered, and legends of Jack she had heard,
but never saw that old sea dog again.

The rain was coming down hard, and Zeke was quite jarred
by Fanny's eye popping story of strife,
so he said his good nights and then scaled the heights
to the roof and his boring dry life.

But an unfamiliar scent slowed his chiminial descent.
It reached his whiskers and got Zeke's mind turning.
Twas like hot without the dog, or *cruisses de grenouille* without the frog,
and he thought, "Where there's smoke, a fire's likely burning."

Sure enough, down below, the fireplace blazed aglow;
blocking Zeke's way to safety and leisure,
so he caught up with Fanny, headed home to her granny—
Unnervingly, she smiled just like a Cheshire.

STRIPE SIX: IN-LAWS AND OUTLAWS

The coyotes sounded closer, and louder and bolder,
so Zeke hastened through the rain to Fanny's den.
When Zeke looked around at the muddy big hole in the ground,
he longed for mother's lap once again.

All around in that cave (or that hole or that hovel),
he saw yellow eyes staring, unblinking.
There were hungry old gran cats and hungry wee kit cats,
and Zeke knew his pirate plans needed rethinking.

First of all, they were big (and this wasn't a dig—
he'd always thought Fanny's size a great plus).
But the matter of tails—or lack of—on these whales
was an issue he hoped to discuss.

"This meal's hardly enough," Granny said, rather gruff,
"and we've waited so long for a taste."
Then before Zeke could question 'bout tails or digestion,
she pounced on him in vicious embrace.

"Granny," Zeke shouted, shaking her off,
"I'm afraid that there's been some mistake.
There's no need to riot; I'm a not a meal but a *pirate*.
May I instead, suggest some chicken or steak?"

"Well there's an idea," Granny said with a sneer.
"We could all use a serving of roast.
And pirate, did you say? A predator and not prey?
I'm afraid, I've been a terrible host!

"If you mean to feed this group, outside's a chicken coop,
and Fanny mentioned you know the way inside.
For a leg, breast, and wing, you will be made our king!"
Granny gave him a moment to decide.

"But what if I fail?" Zeke said, going pale.
Licking her whiskers, Granny responded, "Oh well, then,
if at first you don't succeed, a hot meal is all we need.
We will eat you instead of the brown hen."

Now you might be concerned 'bout the way the plot's turned,
Pirate King after all, is its title.
But please do not frown; there are many ways to win a crown.
Our furry hero is not homicidal.

To catcalls and boo-hissing 'bout the meal they were missing,
Zeke slunk back outside into foul weather
followed by his ex-best gal and her two tough-cat tom-pals.
They would all go birdnap Brownie together.

Zeke marched through the rain, too angry to complain
about the extent of fair Fanny's duplicity.
He was quite stricken: even if he handed over the chicken,
he could trust these degene-cats to eat him, implicitly.

Before he could ponder his dilemma any longer
he felt the wind nip at his sixth stripe.
But it wasn't the cold that had been so bold,
'twas them bobcats (he began to really dislike!)

Zeke mewed,
"What of our deal, the hen I'm to steal, the pirate's code, and
honor among crooks?"
Tired of eating bugs, said the sly one, "We're thugs, and frankly,
between us, off the books…

"Just ask your signora, this desert's the Sonora.
There's no high sea, not for nautical miles.
It's all been an act, no pirates, no Cap'n Jack,
only Fanny's appetite and her feminine wiles."

Stripes Five and Four: The Banditos

One look at Fanny told him 'twas true,
that bobcat was a shrew:
Oh rather he chose to be henpecked!
He just wanted some thrills, not to push up daffodils,
but hindsight is only quite right in retrospect.

The slow cat came from the left, the sly one from the right
and our Fanny just sat looking pretty.
Suddenly from the back, three coyotes joined the attack,
then the night took a grim turn for our kitty.

"The most infamous of trios, we're called the Banditos,"
the coyotes announced to their prey.
"We'll cheat and we'll lie, and we'll laugh as you cry,
then we'll eat you, despite the cliche!"

Zeke squealed an appeal to the mice on the hill,
as a coyote nabbed stripes five and four.
Recalling his history of vice, the mice left him to roll the dice.
He'd've shot snake eyes, had not a miracle occurred.

It wasn't a *deus*—more akin to a small goose—
anyway *ex machina* it descended
from the sky (or the roof of our old chicken coop).
It was Brownie! The effect was quite splendid!

Chickens can't really fly, but she gave it the old college try
and tossed in a bit of heave-ho and some wellie.
With a lopsided lift-off, she carried poor Zeke off
suspended by scruff and his belly.

The Banditos felt confused, and their egos were bruised
making promises they failed to deliver,
but they quickly reloaded their speech and requoted,
then chased those mean bobcats downriver.

Stripe Three: Discrimination

Weeped Zeke, "All is lost," back safe in Brownie's nest box.
"What a fool, chasing fortune and greatness.
I've sacrificed my tail to no avail, lived in pain for no gain,
and turned my safe life straight into a great mess."

"You fell for a charmer, and you're learning 'bout karma
Mistakes will be made that's expected.
But," Brownie remarked, "you followed your heart,
and that quality's most highly respected.

"Why the pirate's route you chose? Only your soul knows,
and you steered by its star, guaranteed.
Those landlubbers don't ken a thing; let's show them who's king!
About now the coyotes'll have them all treed."

Zeke bucked up and rallied just in time for our finale,
with three stripes left in his dwindling lifespan.
"I'll lay them all down," he said, "but for glory, not the crown."
And so the chicken and cat hatched a plan.

Every sailor knows best, the view from the crow's nest
of any tall ship or squat henhouse
is ideal for reconnaissance, while remaining anonymous,
so they climbed the coop to discern Fanny's whereabouts.

When they climbed up, they spied the suspects in a line up,
in a tree, the cats perched all in a row
on a branch fixin' to fall down, in the pool where they'd all drown,
or onto land where the coyotes waited below.

Like a space bird by Brancusi, Brownie dropped behind the jacuzzi
then scooted along the wall out of view.
And like a cat descending the stair, Zeke tumbled with modernest flair
to land in a pose he learned watching Kung-fu.

Zeke spun round and kept on, sword flashing like an electron
then stopped in a pose like Manjushri.
But his blade leapt some orbits (he didn't do it on purpose)
and he left himself with two stripes, not three.

They stealthed round the yard, trying so very hard
not to draw any wild canine attention.
Slipping the kayak in the water to save Granny's granddaughter,
you'd need a saber to cut the surface tension!

The craft was all shipshape, for the attempted great escape
—or rescue, if we're being particular—
except for two holes in the prow, really leaking fast now,
which made Zeke wish he had taken a funicular.

He remembered those fangs, his lost stripe and the pain
and those dual punctures from the rattlesnake attack
the very the night Fanny befriended him.
He thought he had mended them
with kernels of corn (someone mistook for a snack).

Brownie admitted, "I'm the sinner; it's been ages since dinner,
and my brain is all stem, hunt and peck."
"Never be ashamed," Zeke reframed, "of your passions untamed,
but for now, we need all beaks on deck."

So the hen baled and spit–which is tricky without lips–
to keep their small kayak afloat,
while the cat paddled through the gale, using more stub than tail.
Zeke now wished he had taken a sailboat.

"Ahoy," Zeke called from beneath, over the tune of coyote teeth,
"jump in!" he urged the cats, but they wouldn't budge.
"We would no more walk this plank, than jump into a shark tank.
We are certain you must still hold a grudge."

"Oy, scallywags!" Brownie clucked, "you're about to be plucked,"
as the Banditos snapped, yipped, and whined.
"I'm a *tres* busy hen. I won't make this offer again."
The branch snapped before they declined.

Stripe Two: Mutiny!

With insufficient ballast to sustain such a blast,
those fat cats proved they could sure rock a boat.
Plus Fanny cited pride about accepting a ride
despite her inability to float.

To make shaky matters worse, they were traveling in reverse,
and a Bandito dove straight at their port side.
"We've got to skedaddle! Quick, everyone paddle!"
But sadly Zeke's request was denied:

"We don't get our paws wet, or take orders from a house cat,"
Fanny said, "now, me heartie, here's the new plan.
You do the rowing; come on, honey, get going,
and next we'll fry your hen up in a pan."

But Fanny's big dreams of mutiny didn't hold water under scrutiny
for as soon Brownie looked up from her baling,
the bow began going under, coyote ahold of the rudder,
and the soggy bobcats all began wailing:

"Cap'n Zeke won't you save us? Our behavior's been heinous!"
Fanny pawed at her ear tufts and purred.
"You're a fashion plate, a baller, a gentleman, a Rhodes Scholar,
and Brownie, you're such a rare bird!"

But there was no time for knittin' her yarn of contrition,
Zeke was using the force like Skywalker.
Slashing with his sword, he knocked a Bandito overboard.
Sent him straight down to Davy Jones' locker.

Despite wishful thinking, Zeke's pirate fantasy was sinking,
but a sailor, he could still make believe.
Remembering the mice, Zeke hoped his game was cards and not dice,
for he still had one ace up his sleeve.

Zeke jumped and he pounced to get the ship turned around.
He hiked, ran, and reached; jibed and tacked.
On deck was all wild kingdom, but he looked to his wingman
—in position, Brownie signaled for the attack!

And not a second too soon, for under storm and moon,
a coyote grabbed Zeke by stripe two.
But it was all part of their scheme, one last Olympian from the machine,
and from the sky, here he came, right on cue!

The legend, cruel yet cool;
the scourge of seven country club pools:
It was the great pirate Captain Calico Jack!
Shot from the roof like a torpedo, a mountain lion in a red speedo
You're surprised that old sea dog was a cat?)

The Final Stripe: The Fall of Fanny

Jack canon-balled into their prow, before Fanny could meow,
catapulting them all through the clouds and the rain.
Four cats, a hen and coyote; far-flung (and fetched) like Don Quixote,
Zeke now wished he'd taken an airplane!

They came to an abrupt stop, landing on the roof top,
where the airborne strangers looked down for an update.
They saw my kayak in scraps, Cap'n Jack swimming laps,
and the second Bandito quick becoming shark bait.

The last coyote blundered, out-gunned and outnumbered,
surrounded by four mad cats and one angry bird.
Scanning for an escape route, he took a hostage as a way out,
choosing Fanny, which proved quite absurd.

"Step back," the Bandito sung,
but that cat got his tongue before he could sing any more.
Fanny clawed and she spit, bit and she hissed.
Wildcats are not called such for demure.

Steering that spinner by his mustache, despite significant whiplash,
Fanny rode that coyote like she stole it
to the ridge of the gable, just as well as she was able,
to the smoking chimney where fiery hot coals lit.

Zeke had a clue of what Fanny meant to do:
She aimed to roast that coyote like a bratwurst.
But her plan was too dangerous on such a slippery surface,
so he scamp'ed up to negotiate a truce first.

"Stop, Fanny!" Zeke did shout, "We can all work this out!"
But spurring the big boss Bandito to the flue,
Fanny said, "This is for my lost eye. Zeke, don't be the fall guy!
This high ledge is not wide enough for two."

But the Bandito was wily; he schemed all the while he
was bitten and clawed, all snarls and yellin'.
All at once with great force, he swapped ends like a buckin' horse
and launched Fanny from the roof like a watermelon.

Zeke had to act fast, the opportunity wouldn't last
to save Fanny from certain death and decay.
So leaping to commit all, he caught her like a bowling ball
and rebounded her out of harm's way.

As Fanny clung to eaves, the last of the thieves
bared his teeth at Zeke rather grimly.
Zeke didn't hold back, he launched an attack,
pushed that mean old coyote right down the chimney.

To the smell of hot dog roasted, Zeke slipped, slid, and coasted
to Fanny like a cat on a wet tile roof.
As her grip began to fail, he said, "Quick, grab my tail!"
She just smiled without remorse or reproof.

"You must think I'm awful," she said with a claw full
of rooftop right through her nails tearing.
"But right from the start, I loved your great pirate-king heart,
full of kindness, fiery mischief and daring!"

"There isn't much time left, please, hear my last request:
My family eeks by on a pittance.
They need a leader, a father, a mentor... a larder.
If not for my sake, please do it for the kittens."

"Take my final stripe," Zeke pleaded. "No, a king is what's needed!"
Fanny gasped with her very last breath.
Then she without equal, slipped from the steeple
—poor Fanny, she fell to her... sequel?

Zeke rushed down from the roof, and searching, found no proof
that Fanny did ever hit ground.
They scoured the bushes below, but only found a memo
with a heart, said, "I'll catch you around."

47

STRIPE ONE HOLDING: AND PASS THE MUSTARD

Zeke had to smile at Fanny's indomitable style,
but there was one thing left to do before morning.
Though he defeated the Banditos, was the neighborhood hero,
he had to pass the mustard to become the bobcat king.

Zeke said, "Brownie, don't be glum, you know the time has come
to prove your worth as a friend and a mentor.
I made some hard promises, the time of reckoning's upon us.
Now let's complete this distasteful last chore."

The bobcats were so pleased, their hunger to be appeased,
they clapped their paws and their knees began to knock.
But Zeke really surprised them, when he proudly advised them,
"Brownie can use her bird beak to pick a lock!"

To the bobcats disbelief, and Brownie's great relief,
Zeke led them to the door of my kitchen.
Brownie jimmied and pried 'til they'd broken inside.
"We must be quick," Zeke said, "now everyone pitch in!"

The bobcats with obedience, gathered the right ingredients.
The crew was in and out in three minutes flat.
They all worked together, and despite the foul weather,
carried the whole feast back to Granny's door mat.

Oh the smiles on their whiskers, the kittens' excited mew whispers
that their new king had catered in breakfast.
Granny said with a mouthful, "The omelet's delightful,
but this roast coyote, it's simply the freshest!"

When all the bobcats were satisfied, Zeke and Brownie good-byed
(Though the bob-kittens wished Brownie would stay).
The storm mysteriously cleared, and the pink sun appeared
over the mountain, to a bright sunny new day.

That morning, I opened the front door to chicken and cat snores.
They stayed out all night, never bothering to check in.
When he saw how Zeke was dressed, Father wasn't impressed
that he'd rolled home wearing the same clothes he left in.

Epilogue: Freedom

Since that night, Zeke's been different; no longer belligerent,
he doesn't charge doors or nip bums.
He doesn't steal chocolates, he rarely picks pockets
and only borrows dad's car to make chop-suey runs.

No longer a shut-in (though his tail's just a nubbin'),
Zeke now comes and he goes as he pleases.
He spends nights with mother by the fireplace,
only giving the mice a chase
if they sneak in trying to find where the cheese is.

Each morn with a "yo ho ho," he takes his breakfast to go
and sets off to visit Fanny's cuz-kittens.
He sings them pirate melodies, advises against felonies,
and dispenses veggie omelets and wisdom.

At noon, for old times' sake, he slips the kayak past the rattlesnake,
and sails the pool with his mentor and wingman;
then around nightfall, he sits up on the garden wall
smiling benevolently down on his kingdom.

But evenings gazing over the water,
he recalls Granny's granddaughter
and the love that spurred him on to achieve,
and the thrill of the sea—they were all he'd ever need
to feel destiny's pull and believe

that the time of his life was worth all his stripes,
and the freedom he'd won, a wellspring.
Far from domestic or tame, he finally earned his great name:
Tiger Zeke, the Bobcat Pirate King.

All virtue and just two bad things:
pirating plus breaking-and-entering
Tiger Zeke should have gone down in history,
but you can't win *the Walt Whitman* with a poem about a chicken,
so this story will have to stay between you and me.

www.ingramcontent.com/pod-product-compliance
Lightning Source LLC
Chambersburg PA
CBRC092126200426
43209CB00070B/1902/J